CURRICULUM MATERIALS CENTER

ROGER WILLIAMS UNIV. LIBRARY

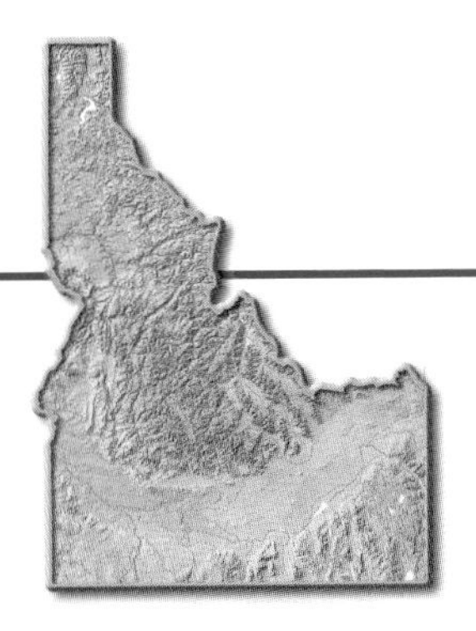

Idaho

THE GEM STATE

by Karen Edwards

ROGER WILLIAMS UNIV. LIBRARY

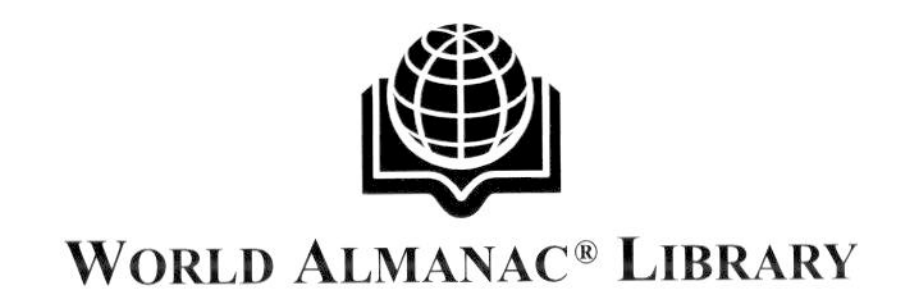

WORLD ALMANAC® LIBRARY

CMC E156 .W67 2002
ID
Edwards, Karen
Idaho, the Gem State

Please visit our web site at: www.worldalmanaclibrary.com
For a free color catalog describing World Almanac® Library's list of high-quality books and multimedia programs, call 1-800-848-2928 (USA) or 1-800-387-3178 (Canada). World Almanac® Library's fax: (414) 332-3567.

Library of Congress Cataloging-in-Publication Data available upon request from publisher. Fax (414) 336-0157 for the attention of the Publishing Records Department.

ISBN 0-8368-5150-1 (lib. bdg.)
ISBN 0-8368-5321-0 (softcover)

First published in 2003 by
World Almanac® Library
330 West Olive Street, Suite 100
Milwaukee, WI 53212 USA

Copyright © 2003 by World Almanac® Library.

A Creative Media Applications Production
Design: Alan Barnett, Inc.
Copy editor: Laurie Lieb
Fact checker: Joan Verniero
Photo researcher: Dian Lofton
World Almanac® Library project editor: Tim Paulson
World Almanac® Library editors: Mary Dykstra, Gustav Gedatus, Jacqueline Laks Gorman, Lyman Lyons
World Almanac® Library art direction: Tammy Gruenewald
World Almanac® Library graphic designers: Scott M. Krall, Melissa Valuch

Photo credits: p. 4 © Corbis Images; p. 6 (top) © Photodisc/Getty Images; p. 6 (center) © Patrick Johns/CORBIS; p. 6 (bottom) © Photodisc/Getty Images; p. 7 (top) © AP Photo; p. 7 (bottom) © AP Photo/U.S. MInt; p. 9 © Hulton Archives/Getty Images; p. 10 © Hulton Archive; p. 11 © Courtesy Idaho Travel Council; p. 12 © Hulton Archive; p. 13 © Hulton Archive; p. 13 © Hulton Archive; p. 14 © Corbis Images; p. 15 © CORBIS; p. 17 © Hulton Archive; p. 18 © AP Photo/Troy Maben; p. 19 © Courtesy Idaho Travel Council; p. 20 © AP Photo/Moscow-Pullman Daily News, Anne Drobish; p. 20 © AP Photo/Troy Maben; p. 20 © Kevin R. Morris/CORBIS; p. 21 © George D. Lepp/CORBIS; p. 21 © Courtesy Idaho Travel Council; p. 21 © Courtesy Idaho Travel Council; p. 23 © Kevin R. Morris/CORBIS; p. 26 © Photodisc/Getty Images; p. 27 © Corbis Images; p. 29 © Courtesy Idaho Travel Council; p. 31 © AP Photo/Troy Maben; p. 31 © Bettmann Corbis; p. 32 © Layne Kennedy/CORBIS; p. 33 © Dave G. Houser/CORBIS; p. 34 © AP photo/Idaho State Journal, Doug Lindley; p. 35 © James L. Amos/CORBIS; p. 36 © AP Photo/Troy Maben; p. 37 © AP Photo/James Crisp; p. 37 © AP Photo/Thomas Kienzle; p. 38 © Hulton Archive; p. 39 © Corbis Images; p. 40 © Hulton Archive; p. 41 (top) © Bettmann Corbis; p. 41 (bottom) © AP Photo/Krista Niles; p. 42 © CORBIS; p. 44 (top) © David Stoecklein/CORBIS; p. 44 (bottom) © AP/Wide World Photographs; p. 45 (top) © AP Photo/Troy Maben; p. 45 (bottom) © AP Photo, Idaho State Journal/Bruce Twitchell.

All rights reserved. No part of this book may be reproduced, stored in a retrieval system, or transmitted in any form or by any means, electronic, mechanical, photocopying, recording, or otherwise, without the prior written permission of the copyright holder.

Printed in the United States of America

1 2 3 4 5 6 7 8 9 07 06 05 04 03

Idaho

Opportunity in Idaho

Idaho had long been home to the Shoshone, Nez Percé, and many other Native American peoples when, in 1805, the Lewis and Clark Expedition crossed into Idaho over the Rocky Mountains. Lewis and Clark and their team were the first white Americans to explore Idaho and discover its rugged beauty and wildlife.

The United States had fought the Revolutionary War and elected three presidents by the start of the Lewis and Clark Expedition. In the late 1840s, the present-day state of Idaho was part of the Oregon Territory, which drew many pioneers to the West. Most of the existing lands later became part of the Idaho Territory, created in 1863. Idaho became the forty-third U.S. state on July 3, 1890.

Idaho's colorful past includes stories of fur trappers and mountain men and lucky gold strikes. The forts established by fur traders later became welcome stops for the wagon trains of pioneers. Some of the early mining camps and timber sites of the 1860s turned into towns that exist today. Others became ghost towns or disappeared altogether.

Idaho attracted hardworking people who had a sense of adventure. Idahoans are still recognized for their independent spirit. From its earliest days, Idaho drew people from a wide range of ethnic and religious groups, including Chinese, Japanese, African Americans, and Mormons. People of Irish, German, and English ancestry were among the early settlers. The rich heritage of Native peoples is also an important part of Idaho's history.

Mountains, valleys, plains, lakes, and rivers are part of the culture of Idaho, not just part of the scenery. In the 1970s, the state began to turn its attention to conserving its natural resources. Environmentalists and industrialists continue to debate about the best way to keep Idaho growing while keeping Idaho beautiful. Manufacturing has become increasingly important to the economy, and Boise is a thriving center of business and culture. In the new millennium, many newcomers to Idaho are seeking a beautiful place to retire or to build a new business.

▶ Map of Idaho showing the interstate

▼ The majestic Rocky Mountains.

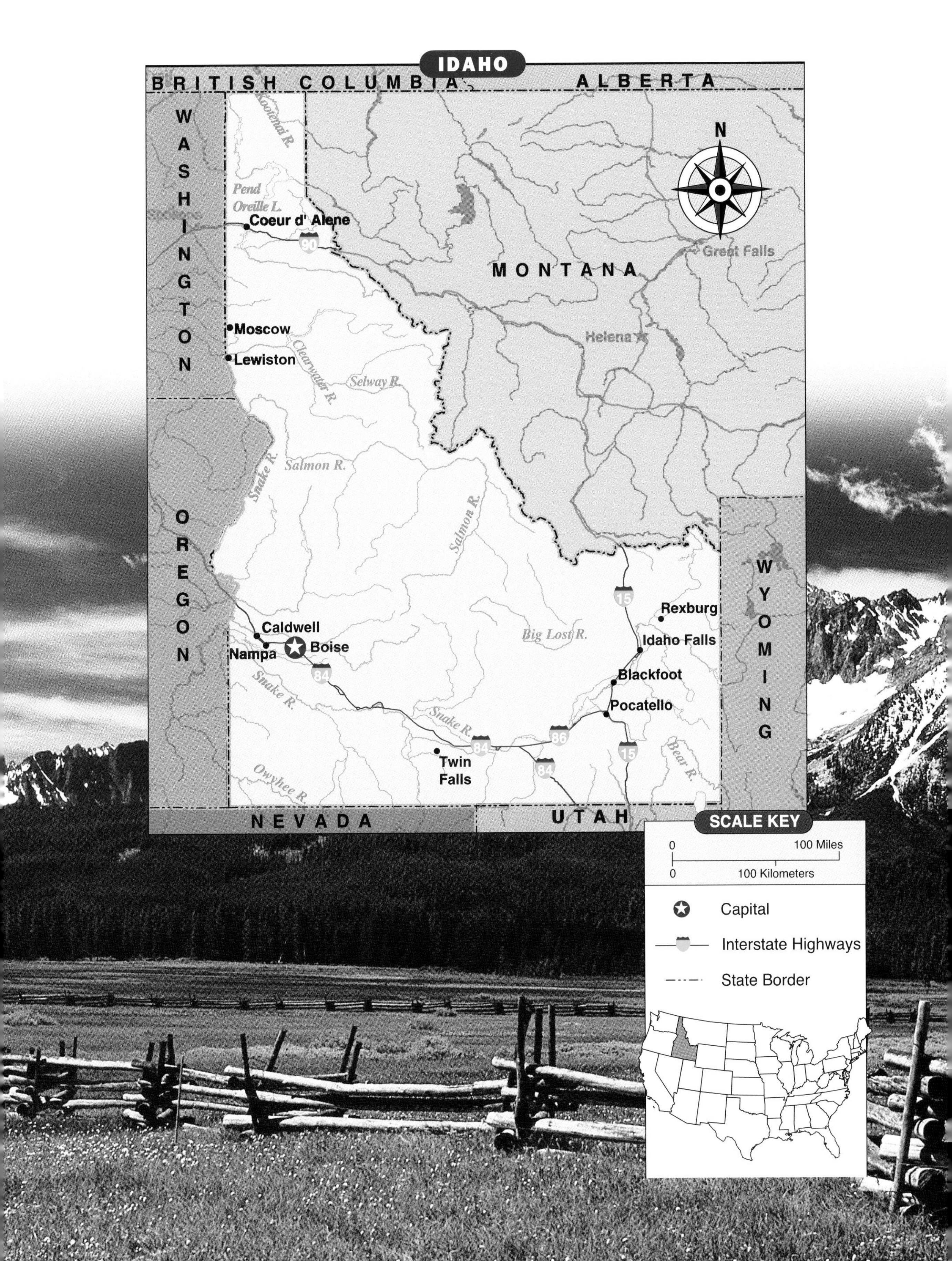
IDAHO
BRITISH COLUMBIA
ALBERTA
WASHINGTON
MONTANA
OREGON
WYOMING
NEVADA
UTAH
N
Kootenai R.
Pend Oreille L.
Coeur d' Alene
90
Great Falls
Helena
Moscow
Lewiston
Clearwater R.
Selway R.
Salmon R.
Snake R.
Salmon R.
15
Rexburg
Idaho Falls
Big Lost R.
Caldwell
Nampa
Boise
84
Blackfoot
Pocatello
Snake R.
Snake R.
86
84
15
84
Twin Falls
Bear R.
Owyhee R.
SCALE KEY
0
100 Miles
0
100 Kilometers
Capital
Interstate Highways
State Border

Fast Facts

IDAHO (ID), The Gem State

Entered Union

July 3, 1890 (43rd state)

Capital	Population
Boise	185,787

Total Population (2000)

1,293,953 (39th most populous state) — *Between 1990 and 2000, the state's population increased 28.5 percent.*

Largest Cities	Population
Boise	185,787
Nampa	51,867
Pocatello	51,466
Idaho Falls	50,730
Meridian	34,919

Land Area

82,747 square miles (214,315 square kilometers) (11th largest state)

State Motto

Esto Perpetua — *Latin for* "Let It Be Perpetual."

State Song

"Here We Have Idaho," *words by McKinley Helm and Albert J. Tompkins; music by Sallie Hume-Douglas. Adopted in 1931.*

State Bird

Mountain bluebird

State Fish

Cutthroat trout — *Native to Idaho, this variety of trout is colored from gray to olive green and has a red or orange slash under its jaw.*

State Insect

Monarch butterfly

State Horse

Appaloosa — *This horse, bred by the Nez Percé, is easily identified by its spotted markings.*

State Flower

White syringa — *Also known as "mock orange" for the delicate scent of oranges given off by the tiny white flowers.*

State Tree

Western white pine

State Fruit

Huckleberry

State Vegetable

Potato — *Idaho is famous for its potatoes, mainly for the Russet Burbank variety, which grow well in the state's rich, volcanic soil.*

State Gem

Star garnet — *This plum-colored precious stone has four or six rays that appear to form a "star."*

PLACES TO VISIT

Sun Valley, *Wood River Valley*
Idaho's brightest year-round vacation spot is in the rugged Rocky Mountains. Visitors enjoy fishing, skiing, hiking, golfing, and cultural attractions.

Paris Tabernacle, *Paris*
The Paris Tabernacle was build by the Mormons in 1889. The builders found the red sandstone in a quarry 18 miles (29 kilometers) from the site and transported it by cart and sled.

Shoshone Falls, *near Twin Falls*
Known as the Niagara of the West, the Shoshone Falls are 1,000 feet (305 meters) wide and plunge about 212 feet (65 m) — which is about 50 feet (15 m) further than Niagara Falls.

For other places and events, see p. 44.

BIGGEST, BEST, AND MOST

- The Snake River Birds of Prey National Conservation Area, located south of Boise, is the world's largest safe haven for birds such as falcons, hawks, and golden eagles.
- Hells Canyon — not the Grand Canyon — is the deepest gorge in North America. At its deepest, the gorge measures 7,900 feet (2,407 m).
- The Salmon River, 420 miles (676 km) long, is the longest river entirely contained within one state. It is known as the River of No Return because of its swift currents.

STATE FIRSTS

- **1914** Moses Alexander elected as first Jewish governor of any U.S. state (1914–1917).
- **1936** Jim Curran invented the world's first chairlifts, which took skiers up Dollar Mountain and Proctor Mountain in Sun Valley.
- **1951** The world's first nuclear power plant was built near Arco at the Idaho National Engineering and Environmental Laboratories.

Thank You, Philo

In 1927, when he was only twenty years old, Philo T. Farnsworth (1906–1971) filed a patent for an invention he called Television System. The young Farnsworth successfully created the world's first electronic television image. This early picture tube contributed greatly to the development of modern television. Farnsworth was born near Beaver, Utah, and moved to Rigby at age twelve. After two years of high school — where his chemistry teacher thought Philo could explain Einstein's theory of relativity better than anyone he had ever heard — the brilliant Farnsworth entered Brigham Young University, which he attended for two years. Farnsworth was inducted into the National Inventors Hall of Fame in 1984.

Who Is on That Coin?

Many people have heard of Sacagawea, the Shoshone woman who served as a translator and guide for the Lewis and Clark Expedition. No one really knows what Sacagawea looked like, so sculptor Glenna Goodacre asked Randy'L He-dow Teton to pose for her so she could create the image for the new U.S. gold dollar coin. Randy'L He-dow Teton is a young Shoshone-Bannock woman from the Fort Hall Reservation. Recently, historians decided that Sacagawea's name should be spelled with a "g" instead of with a "j" as in "Sacajawea." The baby shown on the coin is Sacagawea's son Jean-Baptiste, who was called "Pomp" as a child.

A Colorful Past

Friday, August 5th — We have just bid the beautiful Boise River, with her green timber and rich currants farewell, and are now on our way to the ferry on the Snake River. Evening — traveled 18 miles today and have just reached Fort Boise and camped. There is one small ferry boat running here. . . . Our worst trouble at these large rivers is swimming the stock over.

— *Amelia Stuart, from a diary kept while traveling on the Oregon Trail, 1853*

Most anthropologists believe that the earliest inhabitants of North America probably crossed what is now the Bering Sea via a landmass that connected Asia to North America during the Ice Age. Ancient hunting tools have been found in Idaho's Snake River Plain that date from about 12,500 B.C. Over time, these hunting and gathering peoples began living in caves and rock shelters and, by 1000 A.D., in circular homes. Many petroglyphs — carvings or drawings made on stone — date from this time.

The early peoples of Idaho belonged to two cultural groups. A cultural group is a group of people within a geographic area who share certain ways of living. The Plateau people in Idaho included the Nez Percé, Coeur d'Alene, and Kootenai. They lived east of the Bitterroot Range in almost all of the northern part of present-day Idaho. Plateau people lived in groups, traveling through the canyons created by the Snake, Clearwater, and Salmon Rivers and to areas far beyond. They fished the great salmon runs and hunted game such as deer, elk, bears, and mountain sheep. In summer, most Plateau peoples lived in lodges covered with mats. In winter they stayed in earth houses that were partly underground.

The Great Basin group, which lived in southern Idaho, included the Shoshone, Bannock, and Northern Paiute.

Native Americans of Idaho
Coeur d'Alene
Bannock
Flatheads
Kootenai
Nez Percé (nee-Mee-Po)
Northern Paiute
Pend d'Oreille
Shoshone

DID YOU KNOW?

The name *Idaho* was first proposed for the Colorado Territory, but the U.S. Congress did not approve it. A few years later, in 1863, Congress accepted the name for the Idaho Territory. One of the theories about the meaning of "Idaho" is that it may be a Kiowa Apache term for the Comanche.

The Northern Paiute gathered piñon nuts, seeds, and cactus in the desert. They lived in small family groups, coming together as a community to hunt rabbit and other small animals. The Shoshone and Bannock peoples fished salmon on the Snake River.

Early in the eighteenth century, about two hundred years after Spaniards introduced horses to North America, these animals reached the Plateau people. The Nez Percé became famed for breeding and trading Appaloosa ponies. The Nez Percé, Flatheads, Shoshone, and others rode to Montana and Wyoming to hunt buffalo.

Exploration of the Oregon Territory

The American exploration of what is now Idaho began when Meriwether Lewis and William Clark, heading a group of thirty-one people, first crossed the Lemhi Pass into Idaho in August 1805. President Thomas Jefferson had appointed them to explore the lands that stretched from the Mississippi River to the Pacific Ocean. Jefferson wanted to establish U.S. claims to the Northwest. He also wanted a report on the lands, plants, and animals in the unknown lands. After crossing the Lemhi Pass, the Expedition's progress stopped at the Salmon River. There was no way to take their canoes through the rapids, so they turned back into Montana and went north.

Did You Know?

Many names used in Idaho today were first given by French-Canadian fur trappers. Boise comes from the French word *boisé*, which means "wooded," *Nez Percé* means "pierced nose," and *Coeur d'Alene* means "heart of the awl," supposedly in reference to the sharp trading practices of the Native peoples.

Small family groups of Shoshone like these women and children photographed in 1860 lived in southern Idaho for centuries before the arrival of the first European explorers.

The Expedition then faced the most difficult part of the journey, the eleven-day crossing of the Bitterroot Mountains. Lewis and Clark followed Lolo Trail over the Bitterroots and crossed through Lolo Pass into Idaho in September. In Wieppe Prairie, the team stayed with the friendly Nez Percé people. Chief Twisted Hair drew maps showing that it was only "two sleeps" to the Snake River and five more "sleeps" beyond to the Columbia River. The Expedition set out on the Clearwater River in canoes, leaving their horses with the Nez Percé until they returned in 1806.

Trading Posts and Forts

Lewis and Clark's maps and reports about the abundance of wildlife quickly drew fur trappers and other explorers to Idaho. Expedition member John Colter explored the Teton Valley. The mountain man Jedediah Smith found the South Pass, the gap in the Rocky Mountains through which pioneer wagon trains later traveled. In 1824, Smith also explored Lemhi Valley and the Salmon River country. Between 1840 and 1842, the explorer John C. Frémont crossed the Rockies and mapped the Oregon Trail.

DID YOU KNOW?

The young Shoshone Sacagawea and her French-Canadian husband joined Lewis and Clark in North Dakota. When the team passed beyond the Great Falls of the Missouri River, Sacagawea recognized the land from which she had been taken as a child. During the negotiations for horses with Shoshone Chief Cameahwait, Sacagawea served as the interpreter and realized that Cameahwait was actually her brother.

▼ **This 1807 map shows the route taken by the Lewis and Clark Expedition through present-day Idaho.**

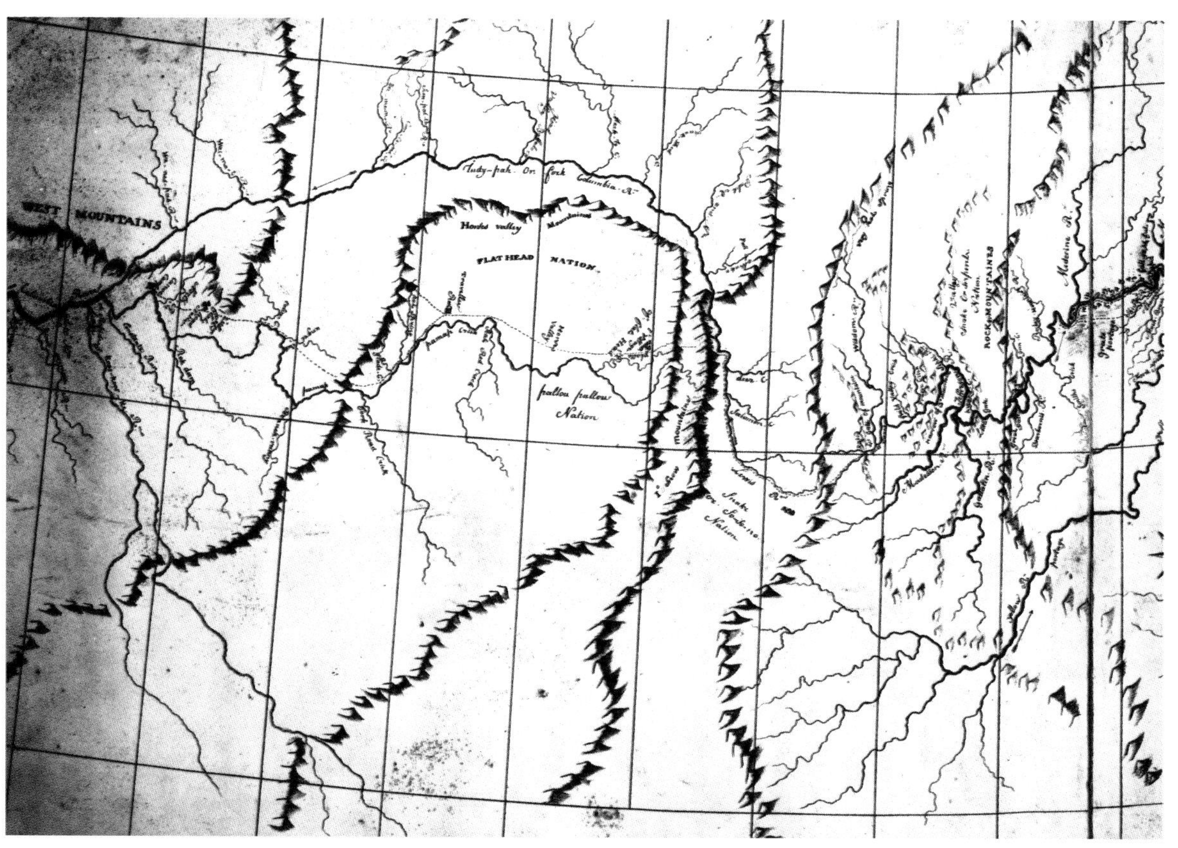

Both American and British fur traders built trading posts and forts in the Northwest. British-Canadian fur trader, David Thompson, built Kullyspell House at Lake Pend Oreille in 1809 — the first such establishment in Idaho. A year later, the first American fur post was established at Fort Henry. Fort Boise was built by the British Hudson's Bay Company near the mouth of the Boise River in 1834. Many of the staff at this fort originally came from the Hawaiian Islands. Also in 1834, American Nathaniel Wyeth established Fort Hall on the Snake River.

New People and New Borders

The first missionaries — people who teach their religion to others who have different beliefs — traveled to Idaho in the 1830s. Henry and Eliza Spalding were Presbyterians who helped establish a mission in Lapwai in 1836. Eliza Spalding was probably the first non-Native woman to travel overland to Idaho. Henry Spalding guided the Nez Percé in farming and started a school. Father Pierre Jean de Smet founded the Catholic Mission of the Sacred Heart in 1842 among the Coeur d'Alene peoples. Mormons moved north from Utah to Idaho in the 1850s. In 1860, they established Franklin, Idaho's first permanent white town.

The news about the good climate, rich soil, and huge forests in the West encouraged thousands of people to set out on the Oregon Trail from Missouri. Beginning in 1843, farmers, ranchers, and workers of every kind traveled through Idaho on the Oregon Trail.

Both the United Sates and Great Britain had claims to the Oregon Country. In 1846, a treaty between the two nations divided the lands on the 49th line of latitude. The British took the land to the north. The United States took the land to the south, which included the present-day states of Idaho, Oregon, and Washington, as well as small sections of Montana and Wyoming. The United States established these lands as the Oregon Territory in 1848. In 1853, all of these lands except Oregon became the Washington Territory.

William Ashley

William H. Ashley was born in Virginia around 1778, but moved to Missouri in the early 1800s. Ashley and his partner, Andrew Henry, started the Rocky Mountain Fur Company in 1822. This company was instrumental in expanding Idaho's fur trade thanks to an ad Ashley placed in the St. Louis, Missouri, newspaper calling for "Enterprising Young Men" to join his new adventure in the West. (The ad attracted famed "mountain men" Jedediah Smith, Jim Bridger, and African-American trapper James Beckwourth.) Fur-bearing animals proved so abundant in this new area that marketing all the pelts became problematic. Ashley revolutionized the fur trade by establishing a yearly rendezvous system — a temporary gathering that substituted for the more traditional trading posts of the time. Ashley became very wealthy by buying the pelts and in turn selling more supplies and gear to the fur traders. Although Ashley retired in the mid-1820s, the rendezvouses continued through 1840. After Ashley sold his interests in the fur company, he became a U.S. Congressman from Missouri. Ashley died in 1838.

Gold and Silver in Idaho Territory

Gold was first found by a group of prospectors led by Elias Pierce on Orofino Creek near the Clearwater River in 1860. Many of the miners who rushed to Idaho came from California and the West, including many Chinese. In less than a year, there were about sixteen hundred gold claims along the Clearwater. The river town of Lewiston became the area's supply center. In 1862, an even richer gold deposit was discovered 200 miles (322 km) south of the Clearwater in the Boise Basin on Grimes Creek. By the following year, the population of nearby Idaho City had grown to more than sixty-two hundred people, and it became the biggest city in the entire Northwest.

The Idaho Territory, which included what is now Idaho, as well as parts of Montana and Wyoming, was created in 1863. Silver and lead were discovered in the Wood River Valley in Hailey in 1880, but the richest silver lode was found in 1885 at the Bunker Hill mine in the northern Coeur d'Alene district. The Coeur d'Alene mines continued to be a major source of revenue in the state into the twenty-first century.

As the towns grew, so did the number of farms. Some miners even gave up their dreams of finding gold and turned to farming the land. Stagecoach lines and new railroads

DID YOU KNOW?

In 1863, Lewiston was declared the first territorial capital of Idaho. The town had been a wild, bustling place with thousands of residents. But when gold was found in the Boise Basin in 1862, Lewiston emptied out as many of the miners headed south for richer lands. The citizens in the south argued that the capital should be where the most people were. In 1864, a resolution was passed to move the capital to Boise.

▼ **Miners pose at the entrance to the Rescue Mine near Warren in the 1890s.**

transported farm goods as well as minerals. From Weiser, the Oregon Short Line connected Idaho to the Pacific Coast. The Great Northern Railroad was completed across the northern part of the state in 1890. When the Gold Rush was finally over, agriculture was well on its way to becoming the state's most important industry.

▲ *Hear me, my chiefs! I am tired. My heart is sick and sad. From where the sun now stands I will fight no more forever.*
— Chief Joseph, when he was forced to surrender on October 5, 1877

Conflicts with Native Americans

A great many treaties were signed between the United States and the Plateau peoples of the Northwest in the 1850s. The United States received vast amounts of land in exchange for very little. Reservations were created. Struggles between the government and the Native Americans could not be avoided.

The Coeur d'Alene, Shoshone, and Bannock peoples each fought the U.S. Army, but the major conflict of this time was the Nez Percé War. Many of the Nez Percé refused to move to the reservation. In June 1877, as conferences between the Nez Percé and the U.S. government were under way, Chief White Bird's group killed four non-Native people. This led to a battle in which thirty-four soldiers were killed. Nez Percé's Chief Joseph hoped to avoid the fighting that he knew would come. He led his people on a zigzag course of 1,700 miles (2,735 km) through Montana and Wyoming toward Canada. All the while they were pursued by the army. Finally, after fighting thirteen battles, Chief Joseph surrendered to the army in October 1877 at Bear Paw Mountain in Montana.

Idaho — The State

The Territorial Legislature had two important tasks in 1889: form the constitution for the state of Idaho; and stop a movement that had begun among people in northern Idaho to secede, or separate, from Idaho and join the state of Washington. By offering to locate the new University of Idaho in the northern section of the state at Moscow, the legislature prevented the secession. Idaho became the forty-third state on July 3, 1890. George L. Shoup was the first governor of Idaho, which had a population of 84,385. Five years after statehood, Mormons received the right to vote, and women received suffrage rights in 1896.

When the price of silver fell during an economic depression, problems that had been brewing between miners and mine owners grew worse. In 1892, some miners

The Road West

The Oregon Trail passed through Idaho for about 510 miles (821 km). After crossing the Rockies at South Pass, the pioneers would drive their wagons along the muddy Bear River Valley, cross the Pontneuf River, and make their way to Fort Hall 300 miles (483 km) across the Snake River Plain. At Three Island Crossing, the pioneers either crossed the river and proceeded to Fort Boise, or took a southern detour and continued west.

dynamited the Frisco Mine near Wallace. State and federal troops were called to keep order. The leaders who were sent to prison formed the Western Federation of Miners to protect miners and get fair wages. In 1899, when the Bunker Hill and Sullivan Company refused union demands to raise wages, a train packed full of dynamite destroyed the South Bunker Hill mill. Governor Frank Steunenberg called in federal troops that stayed in the area until 1901. Four years later, after he was no longer governor, Steunenberg was assassinated by union member Harry Orchard.

▲ Cattle ranching continues in the twenty-first century as an important part of Idaho's economy.

In the early 1900s, the agricultural industry expanded quickly. Federal money was available for irrigation projects that supplied water to the rich but dry soil of the Snake River Plain. The Arrowrock Dam on the Boise River, completed in 1915, was the tallest dam in the world before the Hoover Dam was built.

Idaho's farmers did well after the United States joined World War I in 1917, when there was a great food shortage around the country. Idahoans fared pretty well until the stock market crash of 1929 threw the whole country into the Great Depression. One federal program that helped people find work was the Civilian Conservation Corps (CCC). Idahoans were employed by the CCC to build roads and to maintain forests. (About forty percent of Idaho's forests had been established as National Forest Reserves in 1908.)

When the United States entered World War II in 1941, many Idahoans served in the war overseas. At home, people produced airplane parts, weapons, and food. Pilots trained at Gowen Field Air Base in Boise and at the Mountain Home Army Air Field. At Lake Pend Oreille, men prepared for the navy at the Farragut Naval Training Center.

Toward the Future

The period following World War II saw the construction of new highways and the building of the National Reactor

DID YOU KNOW?

The trial of union leader William "Big Bill" Haywood for the murder of former Governor Frank Steunenberg gained national attention in 1907. This occurred because Clarence Darrow, the most famous defense lawyer of the time, came to Idaho to defend Haywood. Senator William Borah prosecuted the case, but Darrow won and Haywood went free. Harry Orchard was later convicted of the murder.

Testing Station near Arco. In 1951, it became the first facility to produce nuclear electric power. Private utilities companies built many dams to supply hydroelectric power, including the Hells Canyon Dam on the Snake River. The Dworshak Dam on the North Fork of the Clearwater River was completed in 1973. At 718 feet (219 m) high, it is the third highest dam in the United States. In Lewiston, a new port opened inland Idaho to ocean-going trade in 1975.

In the 1960s, some people were concerned that the effects of mining, logging, and agriculture were harming the environment. Others wanted to protect these industries. The election of Cecil D. Andrus as Idaho's governor in 1970 was a victory for conservationists who were against plans to build an open-pit mine in the White Cloud Mountains. Idaho Senator Frank Church helped pass the National Recreation Area Act in 1962. Under this act, in 1976 the Hells Canyon National Recreation Area — which prevented the building of more dams on the Snake River — was established.

Toward the close of the century, Idaho's manufacturing economy became increasingly important and the high-technology industry was thriving. More and more people began to move to urban areas, and the state's population reached more than one million.

Camp Minidoka

After the Japanese attack on Pearl Harbor in December 1941, Japanese people living in the United States were forced to leave their homes and move to relocation camps. Camp Minidoka in Twin Falls was the relocation center for Japanese people from Idaho, Oregon, and Washington. It opened in August 1942 and held ten thousand people. Governor Dirk Kempthorne declared February 19, 2002, a Day of Remembrance in honor of the sixtieth anniversary of the camp and as a time "to reflect on the need for tolerance."

Below: Japanese children attend school in 1943 in Minidoka, the Japanese Relocation Center. The classrooms are in barrack-type buildings.

Growing Fast

> The life and property of our citizens, and those of the Chinese as well, who are engaged in our midst in peaceful occupations, are entitled to and must receive the equal protection of the laws of our Territory.
>
> — *Territorial Governor Edward A. Stevenson, from a proclamation issued at Boise City, Idaho Territory, April 27, 1886*

Idaho's population grew rapidly in the final decade of the twentieth century. From 1990 to 2000, the state's population increased 28.5 percent — about twice the growth rate for the United States as a whole. Boise, the state capital and Idaho's most populated city, gained almost sixty thousand people. Boise is the center of commerce, banking, and government. Many people moved to Boise to join new high-tech industries. New residents are also drawn by the capital's cultural attractions and by its location on the Boise River, with the series of parks known as the Boise River Greenbelt.

Other cities located near Boise also experienced a population boom. Nampa, the second largest city, almost doubled its population. Meridian, the fifth largest city, had

Age Distribution in Idaho

(2000 Census)

Age	Population
0–4	97,643
5–19	316,222
20–24	93,994
25–44	362,401
45–64	277,777
65 & over	145,916

Across One Hundred Years

Idaho's three largest foreign-born groups for 1890 and 1990

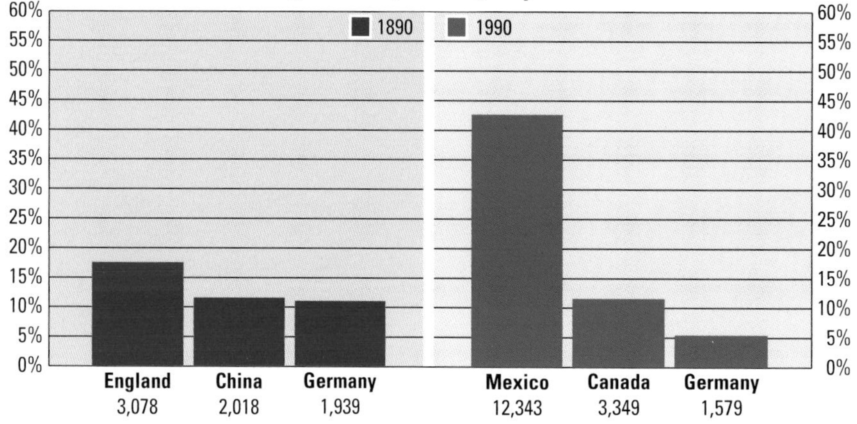

Total state population: 84,385
Total foreign-born: 17,456 (20.7%)

Total state population: 1,006,749
Total foreign-born: 28,905 (2.9%)

Patterns of Immigration

The total number of people who immigrated to Idaho in 1998 was 1,504. Of that number, the largest immigrant groups were from Mexico (65.4%), China (4.2%), and Vietnam (2.5%).

almost four times as many people in 2000 as it did in 1990. Pocatello and Idaho Falls are the largest cities in eastern Idaho. In the northern part of the state, Coeur d'Alene is the most populated city, followed by Lewiston and Moscow.

Urban areas grew twice as fast as rural areas between 1990 and 2000. Nevertheless, the percentage of the urban population is just slightly over half (57.4 percent) of the rural population, and Idaho is still one of the least urbanized states in the nation. The state currently has 208 cities with a population of five thousand or more. The average population density, or the number of people living within a square mile land area, is about 15.6 people per square mile (6 people per sq km).

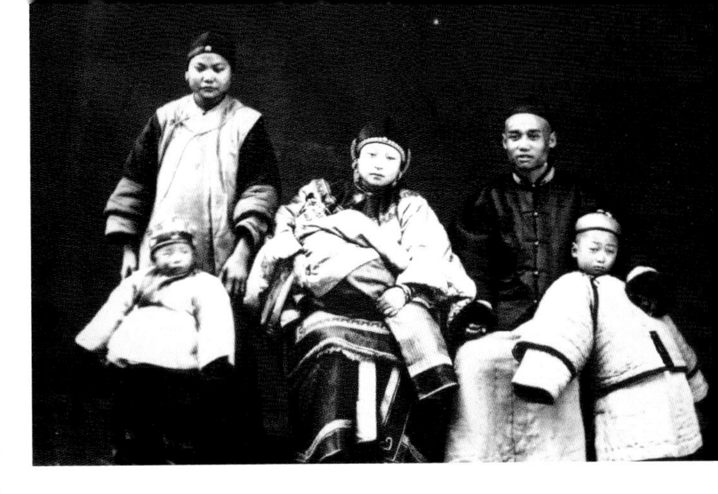

▲ Many Chinese people worked in Idaho's mines. This family came in 1890.

DID YOU KNOW?

According to the 2000 Census, more than one-third of the state's population lives within the Metropolitan Statistical Area (MSA) identified as Boise City. This area, which includes the city of Boise, Ada County, and Canyon County, was the seventh fastest-growing MSA in the U.S.

Ethnic Groups

Idaho's population began growing rapidly in the 1860s when Americans, Europeans, Chinese, Japanese, French Canadians, and others came to Idaho to mine, cut timber, or farm. A majority of miners in the 1870s were Chinese. In 1890, about 40 percent of Idaho's immigrants were European, mainly from England and Germany. The next largest group was Chinese, who were 12 percent of the immigrant population. Several thousand Japanese laborers also worked in Idaho on the railroads at this time. In the

Heritage and Background, Idaho **Year 2000**

▶ Here's a look at the racial backgrounds of Idahoans today. Idaho ranks forty-eighth among all U.S. states with regard to African Americans as a percentage of the population.

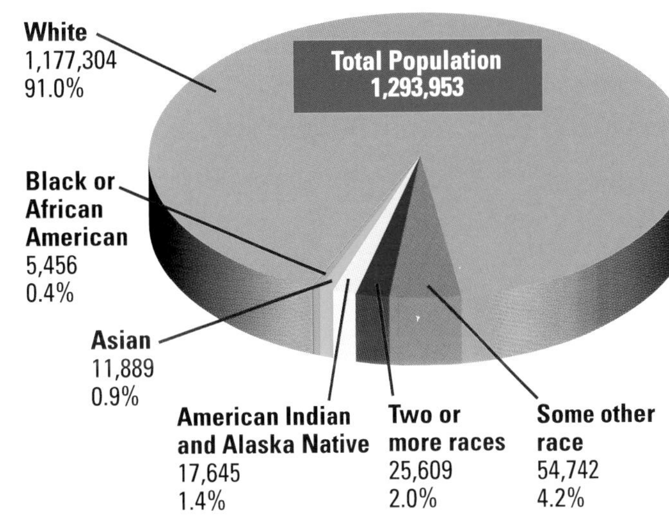

Note: 7.9% (101,690) of the population identify themselves as **Hispanic** or **Latino,** a cultural designation that crosses racial lines. Hispanics and Latinos are counted in this category as well as the racial category of their choice.

year 2000, the great majority of Idaho's population was of European descent, with large numbers of people citing English, German, and Irish forebears. The percentage of Chinese residents is now only 0.2 percent.

At the time of white settlement, the Native American population was estimated at eight thousand. Today, Native Americans together with Alaska Natives make up 1.4 percent (17,645 people) of the population. Many of Idaho's Native Americans live on one of four reservations: Fort Hall, Duck Valley, Nez Percé, and Coeur d'Alene.

Seventy-nine thousand Mexicans make up the largest group of the growing Hispanic and Latino population. Many Mexicans live in the Nampa-Caldwell area. In 1870, only about sixty native Mexicans lived in the area. Some of the

Educational Levels of Idaho Workers (age 25 and over)	
Less than 9th grade	41,039
9th to 12th grade, no diploma	79,322
High school graduate, including equivalency	224,322
Some college, no degree or associate degree	272,207
Bachelor's degree	116,901
Graduate or professional degree	53,714

▼ The skyline of Boise, Idaho's capital and largest city.

early Mexican immigrants were *vaqueros*, or cowboys, while others worked as miners.

Some African Americans settled in Pocatello after working on the railroads in the 1880s. The 1890 Census counted 201 African Americans. In 2000, the African-American population in Idaho was one of the smallest in the nation, accounting for 0.4 percent of the state's people.

Idaho hosts the largest Basque community in the United States. The Basques came to Idaho from the Pyrenees Mountains of Spain and France in the late 1890s. Many worked as sheepherders here, as they had in the Pyrenees. The Basque community is based in Boise and maintains many of its cultural traditions.

▲ The Paris Tabernacle in Paris. This Mormon house of worship holds three thousand people.

Religion

The four largest religious groups in Idaho are Mormons, Roman Catholics, Baptists, and Methodists. The 1990 Census showed that 30.5 percent of Idahoans who claimed a religion were Mormons. The second-largest group was Roman Catholics at 11.5 percent. Mormons, who first migrated to southeastern Idaho in the 1850s, are still the majority in that area. Relations between Mormons and others have not always been easy, largely because their religion once allowed the practice of polygamy (having more than one spouse). Native American religions, Judaism, and Asian religions are also practiced in Idaho.

Education

Idaho's first school was Henry Spalding's missionary school for Nez Percé children in Lapwai, in 1837. The Idaho Territory legislature began planning for a statewide school system in 1864. The state now has 273 elementary schools and 226 secondary schools. The University of Idaho in Moscow was established in 1889. There now are eleven state colleges and universities in Idaho, including Boise State University, the largest school. Private colleges include Northwest Nazarene University and Brigham Young University–Idaho in Rexburg. In 2000, 77,392 students attended college or graduate school in Idaho.

The Chinese Temple

Many of the Chinese miners who went to Lewiston in the 1860s originally came from the Toishan district of southern China. This is a rural area in the delta of the Chu Jiang River (Pearl River). In Lewiston, the Chinese built a temple where they could practice their religion. They believed in a form of Taoism, a religion that includes traditional folk practices and mythology. The first temple burned down in 1875. It was soon rebuilt, and a new temple was later constructed on C Street, which remained there until 1959.

Mountains, Rivers, and Plateau

> I never knew a man who felt self-important in the morning after spending the night in the open on an Idaho mountainside under a star-studded sky.
> – *Senator Frank Church, Commencement Address at Ricks College, May 8, 1961*

Idaho is the eleventh largest state, with a total land area of 82,747 square miles (213,315 sq km). The northern Panhandle is much narrower than the land in the south, so the shape of the state is roughly triangular. Idaho includes three geographic regions: the Rocky Mountains, the Columbia Plateau, and the Basin and Range Province.

Highest Point
Borah Peak
12,662 feet (3,859 m) above sea level

The Rocky Mountains

The mighty ranges of the Rocky Mountains form the state's largest region. People say they form the "heart" of the state. The mountains cover the northern Panhandle and a broad area between the eastern and western borders in the central part of the state. A much smaller section of the Rockies lies in the extreme southeastern corner of the state.

The Bitterroot Range lies on much of the eastern border with Montana. A series of mountain ranges fold into each other in the central part of the state. The Lost River Range includes the state's highest point, Borah Peak, at 12,662 feet (3,859 m). The jagged Sawtooth Range is sometimes

▼ *From left to right:* The Sawtooth Mountain Range; a golden eagle in the Birds of Prey National Conservation Area; ponderosa pine forest in the Clearwater Mountains; Bruneau Dunes; the graceful pronghorn; the Snake River.

called the American Alps because of the beauty of the snow-capped mountains. The Sawtooth Range has forty peaks higher than 10,000 feet (3,048 m). North of the Sawtooths are the Salmon River Mountains, including the bare Bighorn Crags, and the Clearwater Mountains.

Within the mountains are hundreds of alpine lakes and the headwaters of four major rivers, the Salmon River, Payette River, Boise River, and Big Wood River. The temperatures in the canyons, gorges, and river valleys are milder than those at higher elevations.

The Panhandle includes some of the largest of Idaho's two thousand lakes. Thanks to the winds that blow from the Pacific, the Panhandle is mild in spite of its northern location.

Average January temperature
Boise: 29°F (-1.7°C)
Coeur d'Alene: 28.4°F (-2.0°C)

Average July temperature
Boise: 74°F (23.3°C)
Coeur d'Alene: 69°F (20.5°C)

Average yearly rainfall
Boise: 12 inches (30.5 cm)
Coeur d'Alene: 25 inches (63.5 cm)

Average yearly snowfall
Boise: 16 inches (40.6 cm)
Coeur d'Alene: 47.5 inches (120.7 cm)

The Columbia Plateau

Most of Idaho's plateau region lies south of the Rockies, where it follows the curve of the Snake River Plain. The level land of the plateau was originally formed by lava flows. The Snake River aquifer, an underground reservoir, lies under much of the plain. The climate of the plain is mild because it lies between the foothills of the mountains and the desert to the south. Farmers on the plain use irrigation to raise potatoes, beans, and sugar beets. A smaller area of the plateau lies west of the Rockies on the borders of Oregon and Washington, extending north to Coeur d'Alene. The moist climate in the north is caused by winds that blow from the Pacific Ocean. Winter wheat and several other crops thrive in this climate.

DID YOU KNOW?

As a result of the Borah Peak earthquake on October 28, 1983, Idaho's highest peak grew about 8 inches (20 centimeters).

The Basin and Range Province

Southeast of the Snake River Plain is the part of Idaho that lies in the Basin and Range Province. (This region is sometimes identified as the Great Basin Region.) Desertlike basins of sand and gravel lie in between mountain ranges.

Largest Lakes

Lake Pend Oreille
94,720 acres (38,333 hectares)

Bear Lake
71,689 acres (29,013 ha)

Lake Coeur d'Alene
31,872 acres (12,899 ha)

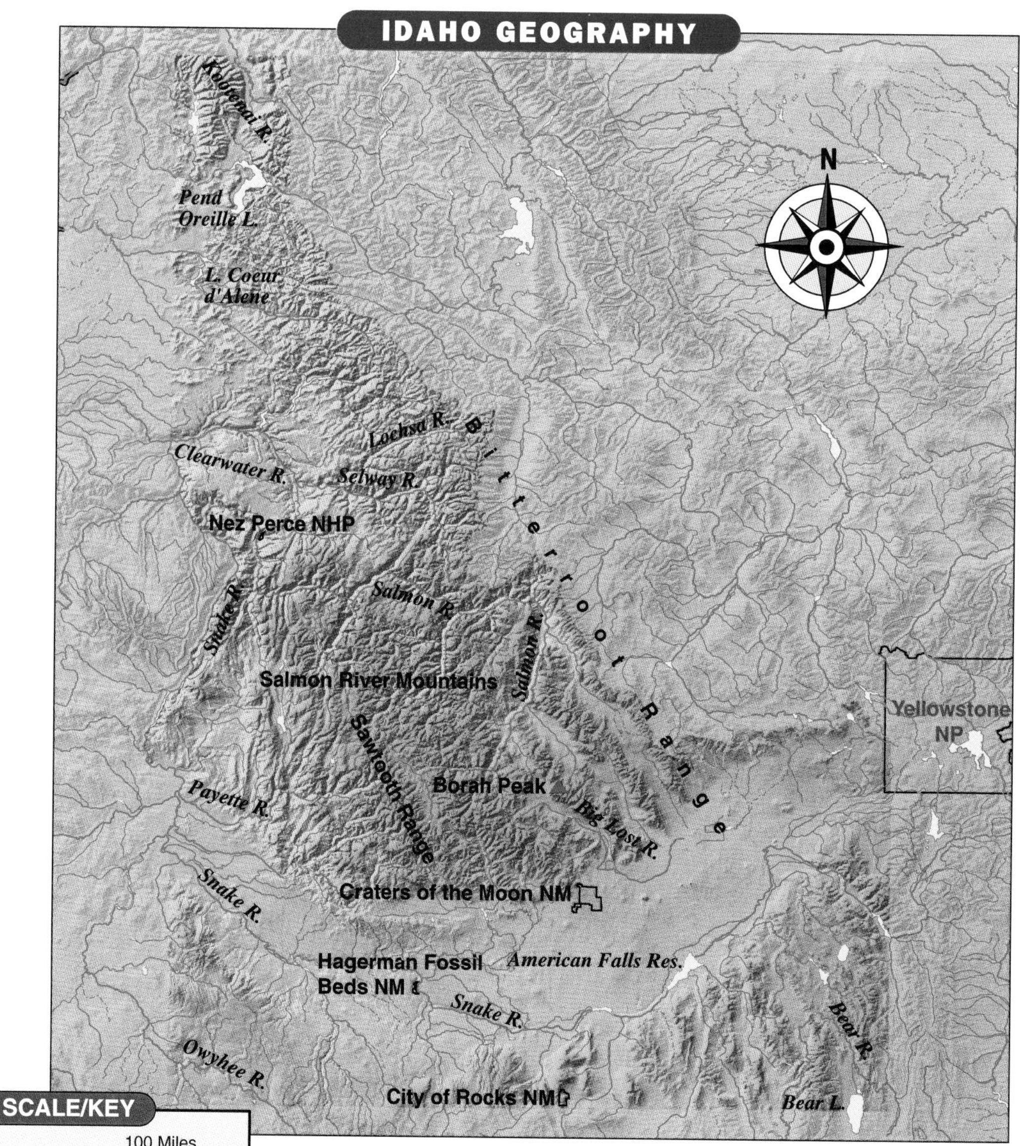

SCALE/KEY

0 100 Miles
0 100 Kilometers

NHP	National Historical Park
NM	National Monument
NP	National Park
▲	Highest Point
	Mountains

Other areas are covered by grasses and sagebrush or fertile soil. The climate is drier and colder than on the plateau.

Forests, Vegetation, and Wildlife

About 40 percent of Idaho's land is forest. The Panhandle has dense forests of hemlocks and western white pine and some groves of ancient red cedars that are about two thousand years old. Large stands of ponderosa pine and Douglas fir cover the Boise National Forest. Other trees include lodgepole pine, white fir, Engelmann spruce, birch, and cottonwood.

Grasses and sagebrush grow in the dry areas in the south. Blankets of wildflowers, including columbine, larkspur, and lilies grow in mountain meadows and valleys. Shrubs like huckleberry, purple heather, and dogwood also grow at these altitudes.

Besides being valuable themselves, the forests provide a habitat for wildlife. Large mammals still find their home in Idaho's mountains. The reintroduction and management of grizzly bears in Idaho continues to be a controversial subject. There are also populations of black bears, moose, white-tailed deer, bighorn sheep, and mountain goats. Elk frequent the highland meadows. In the cat family, cougars and lynx are rare, while short-tailed bobcats are common. Mule deer, coyotes, and sheep live in many habitats. The speedy pronghorn, a unique species that resembles an antelope, live in the dry sagebrush plains. Beavers, otters, mink, and raccoon are common river animals.

The Snake River Birds of Prey National Conservation Area near Boise protects birds such as eagles, hawks, and falcons. Bald eagles can be seen near rushing streams in the north. Geese, egrets, herons, ducks, and other water birds find their way to lake and rivers. Idaho's rivers, streams, and lakes are full of fish, although the salmon runs of Native American times no longer occur. Bass, perch, and many species of trout swarm the rivers. Freshwater salmon and pike are found in the northern lakes.

Major Rivers

Snake River	1,038 miles (1,670 km)
Salmon River	420 miles (676 km)
Clearwater River	189 miles (304 km)

▼ Lake Coeur d'Alene is considered one of the most beautiful lakes in the world.

High Tech, Silver — and Potatoes

> If the government will only aid, even in a very limited manner, the enterprise of her citizens I am fully convinced that we shall shortly derive the benefits of a most lucrative trade from this source [fur] and that in the course of ten or twelve years a tour across the continent will be undertaken by individuals with as little concern as a voyage across the Atlantic is at present.
>
> – *Meriwether Lewis, Report to Thomas Jefferson, 1806*

The story of Idaho's early history also reveals a lot about Idaho's early economy. When the prospectors found gold, Idaho's mining industry was born. The loggers who followed helped develop Idaho's timber industry. In the 1860s, small farms in Treasure Valley, formed by the rich lands of the Boise, Payette, and Snake Rivers, produced food for the miners. Cattle ranches with large herds were already well established in the 1880s.

Irrigation projects turned the arid land of the Snake River Plain into a thriving agricultural area in the early 1900s. A U.S. law in 1895 had allowed the use of public water for irrigation. The National Reclamation Act of 1902 provided federal money for irrigation projects, which led to the construction of a canal system in 1905 that irrigated large areas around the Middle Snake River. The first dam on the Snake River, Minidoka Dam, was completed in 1906 and irrigated a large area. Many more dams were built along the Snake River through the late 1960s.

Manufacturing replaced agriculture as Idaho's leading industry in the 1970s. The production of airplane parts and wood products, as well as food processing, were the most valuable industries before the high-technology industry boomed in the 1990s.

Top Employers
(of workers age sixteen and over)

Sector	Percent
Services	39.7%
Wholesale and retail trade	16.2%
Manufacturing	13.1%
Construction	8.1%
Transportation, communications, and other public utilities	7.0%
Agriculture, forestry, fisheries, and mining	5.8%
Finance, insurance, and real estate	5.1%
Federal, state, and local government (including military)	5.1%

IDAHO ECONOMY
Kootenai R.
Pend Oreille L.
Coeur d' Alene
Moscow
Lewiston
Clearwater R.
Selway R.
Salmon R.
Snake R.
Salmon R.
Caldwell
Nampa
Boise
Big Lost R.
Rexburg
Idaho Falls
Blackfoot
Pocatello
Snake R.
Snake R.
Twin Falls
Owyhee R.
Bear R.
N
SCALE KEY
0
100 Miles
0
100 Kilometers
Cattle/Dairy
Farming
Fishing
Forestry
Manufacturing
Mining
Services
Technology

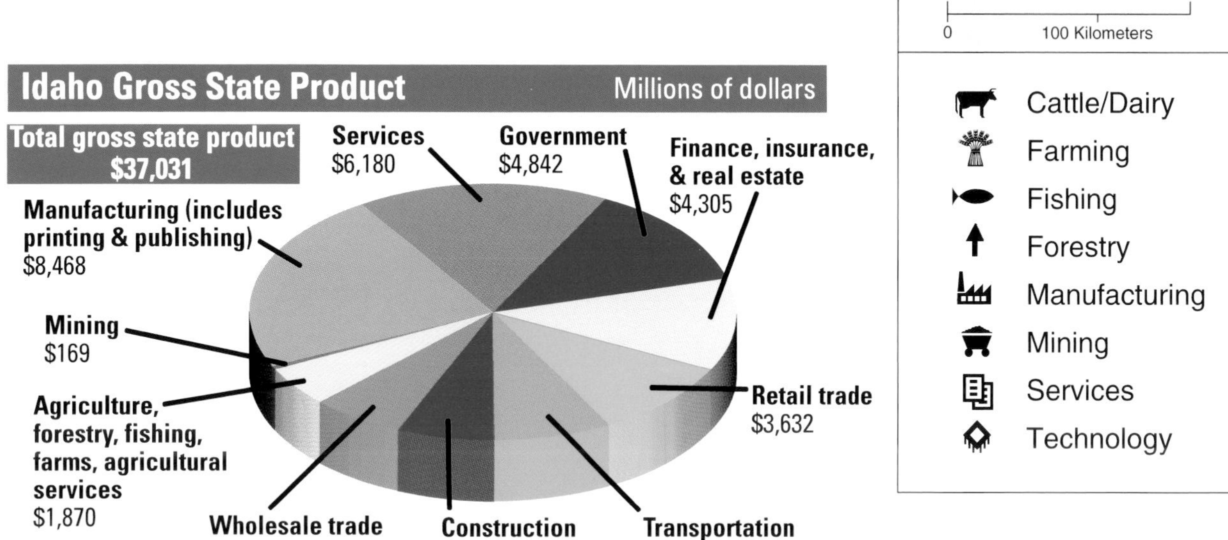
Idaho Gross State Product
Millions of dollars
Total gross state product
$37,031
Services
$6,180
Government
$4,842
Finance, insurance, & real estate
$4,305
Manufacturing (includes printing & publishing)
$8,468
Mining
$169
Agriculture, forestry, fishing, farms, agricultural services
$1,870
Retail trade
$3,632
Wholesale trade
$2,277
Construction
$2,414
Transportation & utilities
$2,874

▲ The Hells Canyon Dam provides both power and recreation.

Agriculture and Mining

In 2000, more than twenty-four thousand farms and ranches formed the base of Idaho's agricultural industry. Idaho leads the country in potato production, supplying about one-third of the country's potatoes. The state's potatoes are so well known that they are called simply "Idaho potatoes." The real name of these potatoes is Russet Burbanks, named after Luther Burbank, who began producing them in the 1870s.

In 2000, Idaho was the third largest producer of barley in the United States and the seventh in wheat production. In the northern Palouse region, the stable, moist climate and rich soil provide good conditions for growing winter wheat, lentils, and peas. Other important crops include beans, sugar beets, and alfalfa seed.

The value of livestock and livestock products, including dairy products, almost equaled the value of Idaho's crops. About two million cattle and calves, as well as pigs and sheep, were counted on ranches throughout the state. Sheep wool is another important product.

Commercial fish farms produce rainbow trout, salmon, catfish, and tilapia. Idaho is the leading producer of trout in the country. The Sawtooth National Fish Hatchery raises over three million Chinook salmon a year.

Although the gold deposits have been largely depleted, the silver in the eastern Coeur d'Alene region remains a rich resource. Idaho produces 16 percent of the nation's silver, and its Great Basin region produces much of the country's rock phosphate. The phosphorus that is obtained from the ore is used in fertilizer. Molybdenum, lead, zinc, and other minerals are also mined in the state.

Simplot's Success Story

In 1928, J. R. Simplot bought an electric potato-sorter and turned it into a local Idaho business. He opened warehouses and become the largest potato shipper in the West. Next, Simplot turned to producing dehydrated potatoes. The Simplot Dehydrating Company in Caldwell quickly became the largest dehydrating plant in the world. Simplot earned a fortune supplying foods to the military in World War II. He next sponsored research into frozen food technology in order to make tasty frozen French fries and built a factory where potatoes were sliced, fried, and flash-frozen. Simplot got the first patent for frozen French fries in 1953. In 1965, he met with Ray Kroc, the founder of McDonald's. Simplot offered to build a factory just for supplying McDonald's restaurants — and thus became part of fast-food history.

Manufacturing

At the end of the twentieth century, the high technology industry blossomed in Idaho. Companies such as Hewlett-Packard and Micron Technology established electronics and computer equipment as Idaho's most valuable manufactured products. Food processing is Idaho's second largest manufacturing industry. Potato-processing plants specialize in quick freezing and dehydration. Other plants include canneries, sugar beet refineries, and dairies.

Idaho also manufactures sheet metal, chemicals, and machinery. The lumber industry produces building materials, paper products, plywood, veneers, and wood pulp. Two of Idaho's largest manufacturers of wood products are Boise-Cascade and Potlatch.

▲ Farmers harvest rows of potatoes with large farm machinery.

Services, Tourism, and Transportation

The growing share of Idaho's gross state product comes from its community, business, and personal services. These service industries presently employ more people than any other section of the economy, and include hotels and ski resorts, engineering and law firms, and private health care providers. Wholesale and retail trade and government services are other parts of the service industry. Boise is a center of the communications industry.

The tourism industry thrives in the Sun Valley area and in other vacation destinations around the state. Tourism expenditures in 1999 were over $2 billion.

About 60,000 miles (96,540 km) of highways and roads connect Idaho's largest cities. Passenger trains serve five cities, while freight trains transport goods. From Lewiston, the state's chief river port, products are shipped down the Snake and Columbia Rivers to the West Coast. More than three million passengers a year use Boise Airport. Idaho's many public-use airports and backcountry airstrips allow access to small communities, recreation spots, and wilderness areas. Idaho ranks in the top ten nationwide in the number of registered aircraft and certified pilots.

Major Airports

Airport	Location	Passengers per year (2000)
Boise Airport	Boise	3,034,354

Made in Idaho

Leading farm products and crops

Potatoes
Peas
Dried beans
Sugar beets
Alfalfa seed

Other products

Electronics and computer equipment
Processed foods
Livestock and livestock products
Lumber and lumber products

Democracy in Idaho

> I take it as a compliment to be known as the first environmentalist governor of a state. I think it's true. I ran as a concerned citizen in 1970. That was the first gubernatorial campaign in America that revolved around protecting portions of the world in which we live.
>
> — *Cecil D. Andrus, governor of Idaho (1971–1977), on the Public Television Show,* Conversations, *November 1, 1989*

The state constitution was adopted by the Idaho Territory government in 1889, almost a year before Idaho became a state. The constitution was put into effect on July 3, 1890, when statehood was achieved. The original constitution is still in use today, but more than one hundred constitutional amendments have been added to it. These additions can be proposed by the state legislature. Amendments may also be proposed by a convention called by the legislature for that reason. In order to be adopted, an amendment must be approved by the majority of the people who are voting on it.

Like the federal government and most other state governments, Idaho's government is organized into three branches. The executive branch enforces the laws. The legislative branch makes the laws. The judicial branch interprets the laws and decides whether laws have been broken.

State Constitution

"We, the people of the state of Idaho, grateful to Almighty God for our freedom, to secure its blessings and promote our common welfare do establish this Constitution."

— *Preamble to the Constitution of the State of Idaho, approved July 3, 1890*

The Executive Branch

The chief executive of Idaho is the governor, who administers the daily operations of government. The chief executive also proposes legislation and carries out laws passed by the legislature. Budgets proposed by the governor are submitted to the legislature for approval. The seven top officials in the executive branch are elected, not appointed. These offices include the lieutenant governor, who is the

Elected Posts in the Executive Branch		
Office	**Length of Term**	**Term Limits**
Governor	4 years	none
Lieutenant Governor	4 years	none
Secretary of State	4 years	none
Attorney General	4 years	none
State Auditor	4 years	none
State Treasurer	4 years	none
Supt. of Public Instruction	4 years	none

chair of the state senate, and the attorney general, the state's highest legal officer.

The governor appoints the directors of departments, such as the Department of Commerce and Department of Labor. Commissions, councils, and boards also comprise part of the executive branch.

Until 2002, there had been term limits for elected executive offices. The term was limited to two consecutive four-year terms, with eligibility to serve again after a four-year period. (Another way the term limit was stated is that the office could not be held for more than eight years within a fifteen-year period.) When the legislature repealed those term limits in 2002, Idaho became the first state to repeal term limits that had been put into effect by the citizens' initiative. In the general election in November 2002, the people vote to uphold the repeal of the former term limits.

DID YOU KNOW?

Larry EchoHawk, Idaho's attorney general from 1991 to 1995, was the first Native American to hold that title in any state government. A Pawnee, EchoHawk grew up in Utah and is a Mormon. He served two terms in the Idaho house of representatives and was the chief general counsel for the people of the Fort Hall Indian Reservation. In 1991, EchoHawk won a Martin Luther King medal for his work in human rights.

The Legislative Branch

The state legislature includes a senate and a house of representatives. In each of thirty-five legislative districts, the voters elect one senator and two representatives. The thirty-five senators and seventy representatives serve two-year terms. The legislature meets every year on the Monday

▼ Completed in 1920, the Idaho State capitol in Boise resembles the U.S. Capitol in Washington, D.C. Idaho's environmentally friendly capitol is heated by a geothermal well five blocks away.

nearest to, or on, January 9. There is no rule about the length of time that the legislators meet, but they usually assemble for ninety days. The governor can also call for a special legislative session. This happened in 2000 when the legislature was called to discuss the deregulation of utilities.

Idahoans often call their representatives "citizen legislators" to celebrate the fact that their legislators come from all walks of life and are not full-time politicians.

The Judicial Branch

Idaho's court system makes up the judicial branch of government. The highest court is the supreme court, which includes the chief justice and four associate justices. All of the supreme court members serve six-year terms. In order to maintain continuity, two justices begin their terms every two years. A new chief justice is elected by the members every four years. One main responsibility of the supreme court is to hear appeals from the next highest court, the court of appeals. The supreme court also hears appeals from the State Public Utilities Commission and the Industrial Commission.

The three judges on the court of appeals each serve six-year terms. Next after the court of appeals are the district courts. Voters in the state's seven judicial districts elect the thirty-nine district judges, who serve four-year terms. District judges deal with civil and criminal cases, while county magistrate judges handle less serious cases.

Local Government

In addition to the state government, Idaho is divided into forty-four counties with county or local government divisions. Each county elects three county commissioners who are the chief administrators of the county. Two commissioners serve two-year terms, while one commissioner serves four years. County commissioners can make resolutions and pass ordinances, or codes, that must be followed. Other county officials are elected for four years; these include the sheriff,

State Legislature

House	Number of Members	Length of Term	Term Limits
Senate	35 senators	2 years	none
House of Representatives	70 representatives	2 years	none

tax assessor, prosecuting attorney, coroner, treasurer (who is also the tax collector), and clerk of the district court. The clerk, who is also the auditor, records licenses and property ownership. Idaho's cities have either mayor-council or commission forms of government.

National Representation

Like every other state, Idaho has two members in the U.S. Senate. The number of representatives in the U.S. House of Representatives is determined by a state's population. Idaho has two representatives in Congress, and for presidential elections, it casts four Electoral College votes.

Idaho Politics

Since 1890, Idaho has elected twelve Democratic governors and eighteen Republicans. More of its U.S. senators and representatives have been Republicans than Democrats, and in national elections, Idaho has voted for more presidents from the Republican party than from the Democratic party. The different views held by land conservationists and industrialists are often the subject of political debate. Idaho's government tries to balance the concerns of both the environmentalists and the mining, forestry, and utilities industries in regard to Idaho's natural resources.

Some radical right-wing groups that hold antigovernment and racist opinions have gathered in remote locations in Idaho since the 1970s. The unfortunate 1992 siege at Ruby Ridge, involving a member of a survivalist group, gathered national attention. Randy Weaver, a member of a white-supremacist group called Christian Identity, had been charged with weapons violations but refused to go to court and retreated to Ruby Ridge. When federal agents surrounded Weaver's house, gun battles killed a federal agent and Weaver's wife and son. After being surrounded for eleven days, Weaver surrendered and was arrested.

Idaho's Great Orators

Two of Idaho's senators, Republican William E. Borah (*above*) and Democrat Frank F. Church, earned reputations in the U.S. Congress for their brilliant speaking abilities as well as for their good works. In the 1920s and 1930s, Borah was called the "Lion of Idaho" and the "Great Opposer." His speeches were forceful and often very long. Church, thirty-two years old when he went to the Senate, was first known as the "boy orator." He earned a national reputation for his keynote speech at the Democratic National Convention in 1960. Church reinforced his viewpoints with funny, folksy stories.

▶ **Thirty-five senators convene in the Idaho Senate chambers at the Statehouse in downtown Boise. At this session, members voted to pass the public schools appropriation bill by a seventeen vote margin.**

A Gem of a State

> If a town can be summarized by a single quality, then perhaps the most notable characteristic of Blackfoot is the fact that its indefatigable [tireless] librarian made . . . this city not only probably the most book-conscious one in the State but also lifted its taste in reading far above the usual levels.
>
> – *Works Progress Administration guide to Idaho, 1937*

Did You Know?

Petroglyphs are pictures carved or drawn in rock with natural pigments. Petroglyphs made by Native peoples more than one thousand years ago are found in many places in Idaho, including Hells Canyon, Wees Bar, and the Owyhee uplands. The petroglyphs may have marked trails or been symbols of people's spiritual beliefs.

Modern Idaho has something to please everyone — music, art, rodeos, and many cultural centers. The greatest thing Idaho offers is its unspoiled wilderness. The state's many national forests, wilderness areas, and about forty state parks are the pride of Idaho.

It would be easy to think of yourself as an explorer if you hiked into the backcountry of the Frank Church–River of No Return Wilderness Area. This region, which includes six national forests, is the largest wilderness area in the lower forty-eight states. The Middle Fork of the Salmon River, which cuts through the region, is rated as one of the top whitewater rivers in the world. More than ten thousand people a year enjoy shooting the rapids in rafts, kayaks, and canoes. The area teems with wildlife. Deer and elk can often be seen on the white sand beaches along the rivers.

Sun Valley in the Sawtooth Mountains is a year-round outdoors adventure. Famous for its ski slopes, the area also offers fishing, backpacking, and camping. In the northern Panhandle, the lakes and surrounding forests draw nature lovers and anglers. Lake Pend Oreille, Priest Lake, and Lake Coeur d'Alene are major attractions.

▼ Rafts travel down the Snake River to Hells Canyon in the Hells Canyon National Recreation Area and Wilderness. Hells Canyon, the deepest river gorge in America, is best reached by water.

▲ Oregon Trail enthusiasts reenact the crossing of the Snake River at Three Island Crossing State Park in Glenns Ferry. Crossing the Snake River here was one of the most difficult obstacles settlers traveling the Oregon Trail faced on their journey west in the mid-1800s. The reenactment takes place annually.

Historical Sites

Idaho's past is alive today at historical sites and local museums all over the state. In northern Idaho, the only remaining underground mine from the 1880s has been rediscovered near Kellogg. The Cataldo Mission, which was built by Catholic missionaries and Native Americans between 1848 and 1853, is still standing. Its walls are one foot (0.3 m) thick. The entire downtown of Wallace, including the old Northern Pacific Depot, is listed on the National Register of Historic Places. The town reflects the life of the old mining days. The legacy of the Nez Percé peoples can be discovered in the historic sites around Lapwai on the Nez Percé Reservation. In the northwest, near U.S. Highway 12, the route of Lewis and Clark north of the Lochsa River is now a historic trail.

In Montpelier, the National Oregon/California Trail Center has computerized exhibits about pioneer life, including one that features a covered wagon. A replica of the original Fort Hall has been built near Pocatello. With permission, visitors can go to the nearby Fort Hall Reservation of the Shoshone-Bannock. The Reservation not only includes the land where Fort Hall first stood, but also Wah'–muza, an archaeological site that shows evidence of a Shoshone presence during the past two thousand years.

DID YOU KNOW?

The Shoshone chief Pocataro granted the Oregon Short Line Railroad the right of way through his people's land. The city of *Pocatello* is named in honor of this chief.

▲ Native American dancers and drummers gather each year on the Fort Hall Reservation to celebrate their Native heritage.

A flood destroyed the adobe buildings of Fort Boise. The fort has been reconstructed in Parma, where a museum is dedicated to Fort Boise history. Idaho City was a bustling mining town in the 1860s. Visitors to this historical area can still check in at the old hotel.

Art, Music, and Entertainment

Boise, "the City of Trees," is a center of cultural activity. Jazz lovers look forward to the Gene Harris Jazz Festival and to the Jazz Saturdays program. The program holds jazz workshops with well-known musicians and presents concerts at the Morrison Center Recital Hall. Live bands perform weekly in summer at the Alive After Five series in The Grove, a popular public plaza. Three blocks from the state capitol is Old Boise, the original downtown. People still go to the movies at the ornate Egyptian Theater, which began by showing silent films. Performances by the Basque Oinkari Dancers are very popular.

The Treasure Valley area of southwestern Idaho has five large cultural centers that present performances by visiting artists, such as Eric Clapton and Yanni, and tours of Broadway shows, such as *Cats*. The Boise Opera, Boise Philharmonic, and the Idaho Dance Theater are top attractions for Idahoans and visitors alike.

Did You Know?

The Idaho State Building was one of the most popular buildings at the Columbian Exposition in 1893. This World's Fair, held in Chicago, was visited by twenty-seven million people. Idaho's three-story building, made of log and stone, was at the time a modern example of frontier architecture. Idaho's furniture makers and artisans contributed to the exhibit. Some of the furniture showed English, German, and Japanese influences.

The arts thrive in all parts of the state. The Idaho Falls Symphony Orchestra performs in the Civic Auditorium. The Pend Oreille Arts Council in Sandpoint presents ballet, opera, and classical music. The town also has a large community of artists and a number of art galleries. Active arts organizations in Coeur d'Alene and Sun Valley sponsor art and music in their areas. At the annual Lionel Hampton Jazz Festival in Moscow, thousands of people attend workshops and concerts by some of the world's greatest jazz artists, such as Lou Rawls and the Ray Brown Trio.

Museums

The Boise Art Museum, begun in 1937, has grown to include more than 34,000 square feet (3,162 square meters) of space. The museum features artists of the Pacific Northwest and modern art. It also has an important collection of American realist paintings — paintings that represent people and places in a realistic way. The Idaho State Historical Museum traces Idaho's history from the fossil age to the present. The Basque Museum and Cultural Center and the Idaho Black History Museum celebrate the state history of these peoples.

Pocatello was the largest railroad station in the region in the early 1900s. The Bannock County Historical Museum displays a collection of antique Union Pacific Railroad cars.

Did You Know?

Many museums focus on a particular subject of interest. The Warhawk Air Museum in Nampa honors World War II history. The Appaloosa Horse Club Museum in Moscow features the history of the spotted horse made popular by the Nez Percé. A collection of gems and minerals is the center of attractions at the Idaho Museum of Mining and Geology in Boise.

▼ Curators at the Idaho Museum of Natural History prepare a fossil display.

The Idaho Museum of Natural History, also in Pocatello, features exhibits on Idaho's fossils and archaeological records, and on its flora and fauna.

A fifteen-thousand-year-old bison skull is part of the wildlife collection at the Idaho Heritage Museum in Hollister. It is one of the biggest private collections in the West.

▲ Les Bock, executive director of the Idaho Human Rights Education Center, stands next to a bronze statue of Anne Frank in the new Anne Frank Human Rights Memorial in Boise.

Libraries and Communications

By 1920 there were ten libraries around the state and now there are more than one hundred public libraries. Two of the largest — the Boise Public Library and the State Law Library, founded in 1869 — are in Boise.

Idaho's first newspaper, *The Golden Age*, was published in 1862 in Lewiston. Today, there are about thirty newspapers. Among the ten daily newspapers with a large circulation are Boise's *Idaho Statesman,* Pocatello's *Idaho State Journal*, and the *Post Register* of Idaho Falls. Idaho has about forty-five radio stations. Boise's station KIDO began as KFAU in 1922. There are also about fourteen television stations and many cable systems.

Idaho in the Movies

Idaho could be considered the movie capital of the Northwest. In the silent-movie era, films like *The Cowpuncher* (1915) and *The Grub-Stake* (1922) reflected Idaho's early days. Among the famous Hollywood movies filmed in Idaho are *Northwest Passage*, filmed in McCall in 1939, and *Bus Stop*, starring Marilyn Monroe and shot near Ketchum in 1956. The town of Wallace is featured in two movies, *Heaven's Gate* (1980) and *Dante's Peak* (1997). The Howard Anderson Idaho Film Archive at Boise State University documents the history of the thirty-eight movies that were filmed in Idaho.

Sports

Idaho's citizens are active in outdoor sports. Hiking, canoeing, skiing, mountain climbing, and competing in rodeos are all very popular. The state is also home to many professional athletes and Olympic medal winners, such as skiers Christin Cooper and Gretchen Fraser.

DID YOU KNOW?

In 1899, a women's group called the Columbian Club began a traveling library system by shipping crates of books to rural areas. The state's official library system began in 1901 when the legislature approved money for the next shipment of books.

The Baseball Hall of Fame includes a number of Idahoans. Legendary power hitter Harmon Killebrew was born in 1936 in Payette. In twenty-two years of pro baseball, he was an American League All-Star thirteen times. He led the Minnesota Twins to three league championships and won the league's Most Valuable Player award in 1969. Vern Law, from Meridian, was with the Pittsburgh Pirates for sixteen years and received the Cy Young Award for best pitcher in 1960. Walter "Big Train" Johnson, of Weiser, was one of the all-time great pitchers. Johnson joined the Washington Senators in 1907 and stayed for twenty-one years, setting records for the number of strikeouts (3,509) as well as shutouts (110).

The University of Idaho athletes who played in the National Football League (NFL) include Jerry Kramer, who helped the Green Bay Packers win five NFL titles as well as the first two Super Bowls in 1966 and 1967. Idahoans Mark Schlereth and Marvin Washington played for the Super Bowl XXXIII champions, the Denver Broncos.

Rodeo greats include Jackson Sundown, who in 1916 became the first Native American to win the World Saddle Bronc Riding Championship, and Dee Pickett, who won the All-Round Champion Cowboy title in the Pro Rodeo Championship in 1984.

▼ Gary Stevens in top racing form.

Idaho Greats

Picabo Street is one of America's greatest alpine skiers. She won the downhill silver medal at the 1994 Olympics. In 1995 and again in 1996, she became the only American ever to win the World Cup downhill title. Street won the gold medal in the super giant slalom (Super G) in the 1998 Olympics in Japan. Later that year, Street broke a leg in nine places, but competed in the 2002 Olympics in Salt Lake City. At age thirty, she retired after the 2002 Olympic games.

Gary Stevens is one of the country's top jockeys. Born in Caldwell in 1963, Stevens won his first race at Le Bois Park in 1979. He won the first of three Kentucky Derbies in 1988. Inducted into racing's hall of fame in 1997, Stevens won both the Preakness and Belmont Stakes in 2001. He wrote about his life in *The Perfect Ride.*

Some of Idaho's Best

All my senses resounded to that sagebrush farm. Never a day passed that I was not thrilled with the changing beauty of the vast cloud-filled skies . . . our gray and green valley, our own lovely, undulating farm, with its ivory wheat-fields, its green beet-fields, its purple-blooming alfalfa.

– *Annie Pike Greenwood,* We Sagebrush Folks, *1934*

Following are only a few of the thousands of people who were born, died, or spent much of their lives in Idaho and made extraordinary contributions to the state and the nation.

SACAGAWEA

TRANSLATOR AND EXPLORER

BORN: *c. 1786, Salmon area*
DIED: *1812 or 1884 (exact date unknown)*

Sacagawea was the Shoshone woman from Idaho who joined the Lewis and Clark Expedition in 1805. Born about 1786, she grew up in the Bitterroot Mountains near Salmon. Between the ages of fourteen and sixteen, she was captured by a party of Minnetaree Indians and traded to one of the Hidatsa/Mandan villages. She married French fur trader Toussaint Charbonneau. Although Lewis and Clark hired Charbonneau as a translator for the expedition, Sacagawea was by far the more important translator and interpreter. Sacagawea was also skilled in finding trails. In the Northwest, more public schools are named for Sacagawea than for any other person. In the 1990s, the United States awarded Sacagawea the title of Honorary Sergeant, Regular Army. The U.S. minted a dollar coin in 2000 to honor Sacagawea.

CHIEF JOSEPH

NEZ PERCÉ CHIEF

BORN: *c. 1840, Wallowa Valley*
DIED: *September 21, 1904, Colville Reservation, WA*

Taking his father's place, Joseph became chief of the Wallowa Valley band of the Nez Percé at about age thirty-one. His father was known to the white people as Old Joseph, so they called him Young Joseph. His real name, Inmutooyahlatlat, means "Thunder Rolling Down the Mountains." Joseph's brother Ollokot was known for being daring, while Joseph was more of a thinker. Chief Joseph was a peaceful leader who was unwillingly forced into the Nez Percé War in 1877. After leading the Nez Percé on a journey of 1,700 miles (2,735 km) toward Canada, Chief Joseph was forced to surrender. The Nez Percé were sent out of present-day Idaho, instead of to the Lapwai reservation, as promised. In 1879, Chief Joseph went to Washington, D.C., and delivered a two-hour speech on behalf of his people. People around the nation were sympathetic to his cause. In 1885, Chief Joseph was sent to a reservation in Washington state, where he chose to live in a tepee rather than in a house.

WILLIAM E. BORAH

SENATOR AND STATESMAN

BORN: *June 29, 1865, Fairfield, IL*
DIED: *January 19, 1940, Washington, D.C.*

William Edgar Borah was the son of an Illinois farmer. He moved to Idaho in 1891 and set up a law practice that represented ranchers, timber barons, and other business leaders. Borah gained national attention as the prosecuting attorney in the famous trial of "Big Bill" Haywood, the union leader accused of murdering former Governor Frank Steunenberg. Haywood went free, but it was generally agreed that Borah had made a better case than the defense did. Borah, a Republican, was elected to the U.S. Senate in 1907. He served in the Senate for almost thirty-three years, becoming a powerful and persuasive leader. He was known for his fairness, honesty, and electrifying speeches. Borah supported land conservation, the graduated income tax, the direct election of senators, and prohibition — laws that make alcohol illegal. He also opposed President Woodrow Wilson's plan for the League of Nations.

GUTZON BORGLUM

SCULPTOR

BORN: *March 25, 1867, Ovid*
DIED: *March 6, 1941, Chicago, IL*

The son of Danish immigrants, Gutzon Borglum was born in a log cabin in Ovid. Borglum left Idaho to study art in San Francisco and Paris, and later lived in New York City and California. Borglum carved the colossal portraits of Presidents George Washington, Thomas Jefferson, Abraham Lincoln, and Theodore Roosevelt on Mount Rushmore in the Black Hills of South Dakota. The heads are 60 feet (18.3 m) high. Starting in 1927, Borglum worked on the project for fourteen years, until his death. His son, Lincoln Borglum, finished some of the details. Mount Rushmore is considered one of the most amazing accomplishments in sculpture.

ANNIE PIKE GREENWOOD

WRITER AND TEACHER

BORN: *unknown, 1879, Provo, UT*
DIED: *unknown, 1958, Utah*

Annie Pike Greenwood never intended to be a hardworking homesteader, but she may have thought she would become a writer. She grew up in Provo, Utah, as the educated daughter of a doctor. In 1906, she and her husband, a farmer, moved to a homestead near Hazelton, where Greenwood became the first schoolteacher. She wrote about

Idaho farm life in *We Sagebrush Folks*, published in 1934. The book describes both the beauty of the landscape and the difficulties of farming, including droughts and poverty. The Greenwoods lost their land in 1924.

Ezra Pound

Poet and Author

BORN: *October 30, 1885, Hailey*
DIED: *November 1, 1972, Venice, Italy*

Ezra Loomis Pound lived in Hailey for only two years before his family moved to Pennsylvania. He lived in Europe between 1906 and 1945. His most famous work is an eight-hundred-page poem, *The Cantos*. Pound's life and work were closely tied to politics. While living in Italy, he became a supporter of the Italian dictator Benito Mussolini, and broadcast his anti-American views on radio during World War II. In 1945, Pound was tried for treason. He was ruled insane and spent twelve years in a mental hospital in Washington, D.C. During that time, he tried to correspond with Idaho Senator William Borah. After his release, Pound moved to Rapallo, Italy, where he lived until his death.

Nell Shipman

Filmmaker, Silent Screen

BORN: *October 25, 1892, British Columbia, Canada*
DIED: *January 23, 1970, Cabazon, CA*

Born Helen Foster Barham in Canada, Nell Shipman began her stage career at age thirteen and sold her first book to Universal Studios to be made into a serial at age eighteen. In 1916, Shipman produced and directed her first film, *God's Country and the Women*. She cast herself as a fearless, independent woman, and the film was a huge success. Moving to Upper Priest Lake, she set up Nell Shipman Productions. There she directed four films. Shipman earned respect for her outdoor cinematography and is an inspiration for women filmmakers today. Her autobiography, *The Silent Screen and My Talking Heart,* was reissued by Boise State University Press in 1988.

Ernest Hemingway

Author

BORN: *July 21, 1899, Oak Park, IL*
DIED: *July 2, 1961, Ketchum, ID*

One of America's most renowned writers, Ernest Hemingway first visited Idaho, where he finished *For Whom the Bell Tolls,* in 1939. Much of his writing drew from his own experiences as a journalist. He led an adventuresome life that included supporting the Loyalists in the Spanish Civil War, driving an ambulance for the Red Cross in World War I, crossing the English Channel with American troops on June 6, 1944 (D-Day), hunting big game, and traveling extensively.

He also lived on a farm in Cuba for several years. A keen sportsman, he later returned to Idaho to live in Ketchum. Hemingway won the 1953 Pulitzer Prize for his novel *The Old Man and the Sea* and the Nobel Prize for Literature in 1954. The Ernest Hemingway Memorial, on Trail Creek in Sun Valley, stands over one of his favorite fly-fishing streams.

PETE T. CENARRUSA

IDAHO SECRETARY OF STATE

BORN: *December 16, 1917, Carey*

Pete Cenarrusa served as a state official for fifty-two years, longer than anyone else in Idaho's history. The son of immigrants from the Basque country of northern Spain, Cenarrusa received the Prestigious Basque of the World award in 2001 for his work in the Basque community. During World War II, he served as a fighter pilot. Beginning in 1950, Cenarrusa served nine terms in the state house of representatives. He began serving as Idaho's secretary of state in 1967, a position that ended in 2002 with his retirement.

FRANK CHURCH

SENATOR

BORN: *July 25, 1924, Boise*
DIED: *April 7,1984, Bethesda, MD*

Frank Forrester Church was a third-generation Idahoan. He became known for his eloquent public speaking during high school. He attended college and law school at Stanford University in California and then returned to Boise. His wife Bethine was the daughter of Idaho governor Chase Clark. Church, a Democrat, served four years in the army in World War II. During his four terms as U.S. Senator from Idaho from 1957 to 1981, he promoted care for the elderly, became an expert on foreign policy, headed the Senate Foreign Relations Committee, and sponsored the Wild and Scenic Rivers and National Wilderness Acts. The Frank Church–River of No Return Wilderness Area was named in his honor.

LANA TURNER

ACTRESS

BORN: *February 8, 1920, Wallace*
DIED: *June 29, 1995, Century City, CA*

Idaho's most famous actress and one of Hollywood's great movie stars, Lana Turner was born as Julia Turner in Wallace. After the death of her father, she and her mother moved to California, where she attended Hollywood High School. The well-known story about her "discovery" while drinking a soda in a Hollywood drugstore is legendary. Even though she was considered a glamorous star in the 1940s and 1950s, she often portrayed an ordinary woman on screen. Turner won acclaim for her roles in movies such as *The Postman Always Rings Twice* (1946) and *Peyton Place* (1957).

ROSALIE SORRELS

SINGER

BORN: *June 24, 1933, Boise*

The compelling voice of folksinger Rosalie Sorrels is unforgettable. Born Rosalie Ann Stringfellow, she grew up in and around Boise. Her CD, *No Closing Chord: The Songs of Malvina Reynolds*, pays tribute to another dedicated folk artist. In addition to performing on her own records, Sorrels can be heard on albums by countless other folksingers. Sorrels and received the Idaho Governor's Award for Excellence in Arts and has performed at the John F. Kennedy Center for the Performing Arts in Washington, D.C.

Idaho

History At-A-Glance

1600s
Native Americans travel throughout present-day Idaho and beyond to trade and hunt.

c.1700
Horses reach the Nez Percé, Shoshone, and other tribes.

1805
The Lewis and Clark Expedition, accompanied by Sacagawea, reaches present-day Idaho.

1809
Kullyspell House, the first permanent establishment in Idaho, is built by a fur trader.

1828
Bear Lake rendezvous organized by William Ashley.

1848
Oregon Territory established by the United States.

1850s
First Mormons reach southeastern Idaho.

1860
Elias Pierce's party first discovers gold at Orofino Creek.

1863
Idaho Territory established by President Abraham Lincoln.

1877
Chief Joseph defeated in the Nez Percé War.

1885
Silver discovered in the Coeur d'Alene district.

1890
Idaho becomes the forty-third state on July 3.

1600 | 1700 | 1800

1492
Christopher Columbus comes to New World.

1607
Capt. John Smith and three ships land on Virginia coast and start first English settlement in New World — Jamestown.

1754–63
French and Indian War.

1773
Boston Tea Party.

1776
Declaration of Independence adopted July 4.

1777
Articles of Confederation adopted by Continental Congress.

1787
U.S. Constitution written.

1812–14
War of 1812.

United States

History At-A-Glance

1890
The Great Northern Railroad is completed across the northern part of the state.

1899
Miners dynamite Bunker Hill mining complex.

1905
Former Governor Frank Steunenberg is murdered.

1915
The Arrowrock Dam is completed.

1937
The Boise Art Museum opens.

1942
Camp Minidoka opens.

1951
Nuclear electric power first generated at Arco.

1970
Manufacturing begins to overtake agriculture as the state's highest-earning industry.

1975
The Port of Lewiston opens inland Idaho to ocean-going shipping.

1976
Hells Canyon National Recreation Area is established on Snake River.

1992
Standoff occurs at Ruby Ridge between Randy Weaver and federal agents.

1999
Dirk Kempthorne begins his term as governor.

1800 — **1900** — **2000**

1848
Gold discovered in California draws eighty thousand prospectors in the 1849 Gold Rush.

1861–65
Civil War.

1869
Transcontinental railroad completed.

1917–18
U.S. involvement in World War I.

1929
Stock market crash ushers in Great Depression.

1941–45
U.S. involvement in World War II.

1950–53
U.S. fights in the Korean War.

1964–73
U.S. involvement in Vietnam War.

2000
George W. Bush wins the closest presidential election in history.

2001
A terrorist attack in which four hijacked airliners crash into New York City's World Trade Center, the Pentagon, and farmland in western Pennsylvania leaves thousands dead or injured.

▼ Settlers made their way through Idaho in "trains" of covered wagons in the 1800s.

Festivals and Fun for All

Basque Picnic, Mountain Home

This August event, held in Basque Park, celebrates the traditional Basque culture with Basque games, artists' booths, cultural dancing, and delicious food.
www.ci.mountain-home.id.us/MH_Arts.htm

Cinco de Mayo, Caldwell

A traditional Mexican holiday is celebrated with a parade, led by *charro* horse riders, mariachi bands, and performances of *téjano* (Mexican-Texan) music.
www.caldwellidaho.org

Ketchum Wagon Days, Ketchum

Every year, Ketchum celebrates its mining history with the Wagon Days Big Hitch Parade, the largest non-motorized parade in the West. Also features Old West entertainment, from pancake breakfasts to barbecues and Western dancing at night.
www.ci.ketchum.id.us/wd_history.aspy.com

Massacre Rocks Rendezvous, American Falls

This early June rendezvous re-creates the meetings between mountain men, trappers, and Native Americans. It features a teepee village, a knife-throwing contest, and more.
www.visitid.org

Dodge National Circuit Finals Rodeo, Pocatello

Watch professional cowboys compete in the second largest points-qualifying rodeo in the United States. Then follow them to Pebble Creek, where cowboys and cowgirls ride down the mountain on a barrel that is roped between two skiers.
www.dncfr.com

Festival at Sandpoint, Sandpoint

For more than two decades, people have looked forward to the music presented on the shores of Lake Pend Oreille by big-name acts in classical, blues, folk, world, and popular music.
www.festivalatsandpoint.com

Mat'Alyma Powwow and Root Festival, Kamiah

Held on the Nez Percé Reservation, the popular May powwow includes contests in traditional and fancy dress for children and adults, memorials, music and dancing, and arts and crafts.
www.idahonwp.org/todo/clear/arts.htm

National Old Time Fiddlers' Contest, Weiser

Expert fiddle players gather in June to celebrate a musical tradition. Take a look at the National Fiddlers Hall of Fame as well.
www.fiddlecontest.com

North Idaho Timberfest, Bonner County Fairgrounds

Competitions in standing block chop, pole climbing, and more honor the skills of the early loggers. Local challenge events like the loggers relay and tug-of-war are big crowd pleasers.
http:sandpoint.org/timberfest

River Festival, Boise

"America's Finest Family Festival" has four hundred free events, a parade of giant inflatable figures, and a nighttime parade of lighted, animated floats. Hot air balloons bloom in the sky all week. A huge fireworks show caps off the festival.
www.boiseriverfestival.org

Shoshone-Bannock Indian Festival, Fort Hall Reservation

Festivities include traditional dance, arts and crafts exhibits, parades, fun run, traditional handgames, and rodeo events.
www.sho-ban.com

Snake River Stampede, Nampa

Nampa proudly hosts one of the nation's top rodeos. Nonstop events include bareback bronc riding, calf roping, and bull riding.
www.snakeriverstampede.com

St. Anthony Cowboy Poetry Gathering, St. Anthony

Hear the greatest cowboy poets, listen to old trail songs, and watch a cowboy variety show.
www.cowboypoetry.com

Three Island Crossing, Glenns Ferry

Horses and riders reenact the historic Oregon Trail wagon train crossing of the Snake River in the Three Island Crossing State Park.
www.idahoparks.org

▶ An artist and his work at the Shoshone-Bannock Indian Festival.

Books

Blumberg, Rhoda. *The Incredible Journey of Lewis & Clark.* New York: Beech Tree Books, 1995. Follow the Expedition as it crosses the Louisiana Territory and the West, including Idaho.

Bragg, L. E. *More Than Petticoats: Remarkable Idaho Women.* Guilford, CT: Globe Pequot Press, 2001. Fascinating stories about Idaho women, including the missionary Eliza Spalding, who played a part in the state's early history.

Fradin, Dennis Brindell. *Idaho.* Chicago: Children's Press, 1995. This overview of Idaho's history includes many important facts.

Ingold, Jeanette. *The Big Burn.* New York: Harcourt, 2002. A historical novel based on the true story of the devastating 1910 wildfire that spread over the Idaho Panhandle. The story, which focuses on young people whose lives are connected through the fire, includes "field notes" about the path of the fire.

Sorrels, Rosalie. *Way Out in Idaho: A Celebration of Songs and Stories.* Lewiston, ID: Confluence Press, 1991. A collection of traditional stories and songs that leads readers (and singers) into Idaho's past in a new way.

Taylor, Marian W. *Chief Joseph: Nez Percé Leader.* New York: Chelsea House, 1993. This nonfiction book includes black and white photographs that help tell the story of Chief Joseph and his people.

Web Sites

▶ Official state web site
www.state.id.us

▶ Tourism web site
www.visitid.org

▶ The Idaho State Historical Society
www.idahohistory.net

Note: Page numbers in *italics* refer to maps, illustrations, or photographs.